Raclette

Contents

Getting Started

The Recipes

Appendix

Cooking at the Table—A Convivial Dining Experience

Even if modern raclette has little in common with the Swiss original, the most important aspect survives: the coziness and leisure of sitting around the table together while grilling and cooking your food. This book provides you with a whole range of possibilities for melting cheese over vegetables, meat, and fish using a raclette machine. A separate chapter is dedicated to the grill (and hot stone) that comes with many raclette machines.

Equipment

1 | Raclette Trays

In another era, Swiss raclette was a very simple meal. Half a cheese round was heated in front of an open fireplace and the melting cheese was scraped onto potatoes, layer by layer. However, that old world method is a bit impractical for most modern households. Today, specialty cookware dealers offer a variety of electric raclette machines in different models and price ranges that fit on any table-top. With any of the raclette machines you may purchase the principle is always the same. The ingredients are placed in small, non-stick raclette dishes to cook under a heating element.

> **1** Use wooden spatulas on nonstick raclette dishes to keep from damaging the surfaces.

2 | Raclette Grill

The raclette machines most frequently sold today have a non-stick grill on top of the heating elements and trays. This lets you grill meat, fish, or vegetables on top while the side dish cooks and the cheese melts in the trays below. Many of the recipes in this book were developed for this type of appliance, which allows a little more variety in the types of meals you can prepare.

3 | Raclette with Hot Stone

Grilling is an ancient technique that as a cooking method is low-fat and wonderfully aromatic, especially when you can cook your meal right at the table. The hot stone is first pre-heated (in the oven or on the raclette machine's heating elements). The heating elements then maintain a constant temperature and can be adjusted higher or lower by a control.

> **2** *The hot stone is a delicious, aromatic way to cook.*

Note

Whatever raclette machine you have, always read the manufacturer's operating instructions. And be careful at the table. Appliances, trays, and the area immediately surrounding them become extremely hot.

Above each recipe, you'll find an indication of the type of raclette machine required, either a raclette with hot stone, grill top, or raclette trays. The recipes that indicate raclette trays can be used with either type.

Ingredients

Cheese

➤ For a raclette dinner, plan on 7–8 oz of cheese per person. Since cheese is the most important ingredient in raclette, we'll introduce you to the types of cheese used in the recipes on the next page.

Vegetables

➤ Tender vegetables can be raw when cooked on the raclette grill, as long as they're cut up into small enough pieces. For firmer vegetables, blanch them briefly until al dente and rinse them under cold water before cutting them up.

Fruit

➤ Cheese and fruit are a classic combination, especially fruit that's slightly tart like those used in gratins and cheese desserts. Ideal fruits include apples, pears, plums, apricots, figs, mango, and papaya.

Meat

➤ Meat prepared in a raclette machine should be pre-cooked or cut up very finely so it will be cooked through-out in a short period of time. Marinating it beforehand makes it especially tender. When using a hot stone, the pieces of meat can be slightly thicker.

Fish

➤ Fish is ideal for raclette because it cooks quickly. When grilling, it's better to use fattier types such as mackerel, salmon, catfish, or filets with the skin on. Peeled or unpeeled shrimp are also delicious on the grill.

Potatoes

➤ Small new potatoes boiled in their skins are the traditional accompaniment to raclette. Plan on about a half of a pound per person if the potatoes are the only filling side dish. Wrap the potatoes in a damp cloth and place them in a bowl next to the raclette machine.

Side Dishes

➤ Vegetables and fresh salads are excellent accompani-ments to raclette dishes. Sauces and dips are essential if you're using a grill. You'll find recipes and ideas in the last two chapters.

Seasonings

➤ Always set salt (preferably kosher or sea), freshly ground black pepper, and perhaps paprika on the table for the potatoes. Grilled foods should be seasoned only after cooking. Be sure to scrape off marinades thoroughly before cooking, otherwise the seasonings will burn.

Quantities

➤ The recipes in this book are designed for 4 people (using 8 cheese trays). This allows you to serve several dishes and combinations. A word about side dishes: If you're feeding more than 4 people, serve several side dishes or prepare larger amounts.

Cheese Glossary

Butterkäse: Semi-soft cheese from cow's milk; 45% fat content; creamy and sliceable consistency; mild and slightly tart aroma, goes well with sweet and spicy-hot ingredients.

Camembert: Soft cheese from raw cow's milk; minimum 45% fat content; creamy yellow; softens with age; rind formed by mold; typical aroma of fresh mushrooms, becomes very tangy with aging.

Cheddar: Firm cheese from cow's milk; 45–50% fat content; white, yellow, or orange; creamy consistency with few holes; ranging from firm and elastic to slightly crumbly; acidic, nutty flavor

Emmenthaler: Firm cheese from raw cow's milk; 45% fat content; ivory-colored with cherry to plum-sized holes and a firm and creamy consistency; mild aroma and nutty flavor.

Feta: Soft or fresh cheese originally made from sheep's milk; 40–55% fat content; white and crumbly consistency; aromatic to sharp flavor depending on sheep's milk.

Fontina: Semi-firm cheese from raw cow's milk produced in the valley of Aosta in Italy; minimum 45% fat content; white to straw-colored with small holes; flavor ranging from fine and delicate to aromatic and tangy.

Gorgonzola: Soft cheese from cow's milk; minimum 48% fat content; cream-colored with blue-green veins and reddish rind; crumbly consistency; flavor ranging from aromatic to sharp and rich.

Gouda: Traditionally made from cow's milk but also available made from goat milk; produced with various fat contents; flavor ranging from mild to very tangy depending on age and type of milk, but always melts well.

Gruyère: Firm cheese from raw cow's milk; minimum 49% fat content; ivory to yellow color with scattered holes; rind coated with a red bacteria; distinctively tangy and hearty flavor.

Manchego: Firm cheese from sheep's milk; minimum 50% fat content; light color with small, irregular holes; when young, tastes relatively neutral, when aged, flavor ranges from slightly nutty to aromatic.

Mozzarella: Fresh cheese from cow's milk; 40–45% fat content; available in balls, cylinders, or bars; white, elastic, and sliceable; with a neutral and mild flavor, it goes with everything.

Parmesan/Pecorino: Hard cheese from raw cow's milk; minimum 32% fat content; hard and fine-grained even after broiling; tastes aromatic and tangy; with raclette, used for grating and seasoning.

Raclette: Firm cheese from cow's milk; 50% fat content; ivory to golden color with a soft and creamy consistency, with few holes; depending on degree of ripeness, flavor can range from mildly fruity to aromatic.

Roquefort: Soft cheese from raw sheep's milk; 54% fat content; white to cream-colored with a firm and creamy consistency and pronounced blue-green veins; the riper the cheese, the milder the flavor.

Scamorza: Fresh or firm cheese from cow's milk; also available smoked; cream-colored, mozzarella-like consistency; flavor ranging from pleasantly fresh to slightly smoky; ideal for melting and, therefore, broiling.

Tilsit: Firm cheese from cow's milk; 30–60% fat content; golden with irregular holes; elastic, sliceable; flavor ranging from slightly tart to sharp, pleasantly acidic.

7

> **1** Pre-Dinner Cocktail:
> Cynar Cocktail

Makes 1 cocktail: Mix 1 oz Cynar (Italian artichoke liqueur), 1 oz white Vermouth, and ice in a cocktail glass. Squeeze the juice from ¼ of an orange over the top and serve immediately.

> **2** Pre-Dinner Cocktail:
> Fino Martini

Makes 1 cocktail: Mix 2 oz London Dry Gin, 1 tsp Fino Sherry, and a lot of ice in a cocktail shaker and mix well. Strain into a chilled martini glass. Garnish with lemon peel if desired.

> **3** After-Dinner Drink:
> Kirsch & Cassis

Makes 1 drink: Mix 2 oz Crème de Cassis, 1 oz cherry brandy, and ice cubes in a balloon glass. Add soda water as desired and garnish with 1 maraschino cherry.

> **4** After-Dinner Drink:
> Grappa Sour

Makes 1 drink. Mix ½–1 oz lemon juice, ¼—½ oz sugar syrup, 1½ oz grappa and ice in a cocktail glass and serve.

Beverages

Cocktails, Wine, Beer

Wine
Light-bodied dry white wines, such as sauvignon blanc, are excellent partners for raclette and should be served at a temperature of 50–55°F. Even fruity, light red wines, such as pinot noir, can be chilled and served with raclette. In Switzerland, raclette is traditionally accompanied by a Fendant, a white wine from the Valais region.

Beer
Beer also goes well with raclette, especially with some of the heartier dishes.

Tip: A raclette machine gets hotter over time and heats the area around it, so don't place beverages in the immediate vicinity of the appliance.

Beverages

Nonalcoholic

Raclette is equally as delicious when enjoyed without alcohol. Either way, you should provide a selection of non-alcoholic beverages—in particular, a large amount of water as a thirst quencher. You can serve sparkling water with freshly squeezed lime or lemon juice as well as several different fruit juices.

A grape juice spritzer goes especially well with cheese dishes. A heartier raclette, however, is better served with a more neutral apple juice or nonalcoholic beer. More exotic and fruity dishes can be accompanied by spritzers made with tropical fruit juices, such as passion fruit or guava. For raclette with an Asian flair, you can also serve iced green or verbena tea.

Pre-Dinner Mocktail: Virgin Mary

Makes 1 drink: Purée 8$1/2$ oz tomato flesh, 3$1/2$ oz carrots, 3$1/2$ ounces celery, and $1/2$ onion, strain, and pour into a glass with ice. Add mineral water and season to taste with Tabasco, salt, and pepper.

Pre-Dinner Mocktail: Orange-Carrot Sip

Makes 1 drink: Mix 2$1/2$ oz unsweetened carrot juice, 2$1/2$ oz freshly squeezed orange juice, and 1 tbs finely chopped chervil. Pour into a glass filled with ice.

After-Dinner Drink: Cranberry Cooler

Makes 1 drink: Mix 2$1/2$ oz cranberry juice, 4 tbs freshly squeezed red grapefruit juice, and 1$1/2$ oz lemon-lime soft drink. Serve in a chilled glass.

After-Dinner Drink: Tropical Mango Mix

Makes 1 drink: Purée flesh of $1/2$ mango, 6$1/2$ oz freshly squeezed orange juice, and 1–2 tbs lime juice. Pour into a glass and serve with lemon balm.

Fruit and Vegetables with Cheese

Fruit and vegetables are a perfect match for tangy cheeses—just reading these recipes will make your mouth water. Dishes such as Rosemary-Infused Mediterranean Vegetables or Figs with Honey and Peppercorns evoke visions of warm summer nights dining alfresco.

Sugar Snap Peas with Truffle Oil

SERVES 4:

➤ 1 lb sugar snap peas | 1 large
red bell pepper | Salt | Pepper
$1/3$ cup truffle oil
$3\,1/2$ oz freshly grated Parmesan

1 | Rinse and clean vegetables. Cut sugar snap peas in half on an angle. Cut bell pepper into quarters and then into strips $1/3$-inch wide. Place both in boiling salted water for 2 minutes, rinse under cold water, and drain.

2 | Distribute sugar snap peas and bell pepper in cooking trays and season with salt and pepper. Drizzle truffle oil over the top, sprinkle evenly with Parmesan, and cook under the heating element for 6–8 minutes.

Brussels Sprouts with Fried Onion Sprinkles

SERVES 4:

➤ $1\,1/2$ lbs Brussels sprouts, blanched
in boiling water | 1 bunch parsley
$2\,1/2$ tbs butter | $1/2$ cup packaged
fried onions | Salt | Pepper
Freshly grated nutmeg
1 lb sliced Raclette cheese

1 | Cut Brussels sprouts in half lengthwise. Rinse parsley, shake dry, and chop. Melt butter and mix with Brussels sprouts, parsley, and onions. Season with salt, pepper, and nutmeg.

2 | Distribute Brussels sprout mixture in cooking trays, top with cheese, and cook under the heating element for 6–8 minutes.

Raclette Trays

Mixed Mushrooms with Cheese

SERVES 4:

➤ 1 onion

1½ lbs mixed fresh mushrooms

1½ tbs butter

⅓ cup white wine (may substitute stock)

4 tbs chopped parsley

½ cup crème fraîche

5 oz grated Gouda

Salt | White pepper

⏱ Prep time: 20 minutes

⏱ Cooking time: 7 minutes

➤ Calories/serving: About 385

1 | Peel onion and dice finely. Clean mushrooms and cut into thin slices or pieces. Heat butter in a pan and braise onions and mushrooms. Pour in wine and boil away liquid. Stir in parsley, crème fraîche, and cheese and season with salt and pepper.

2 | At the table, transfer mushroom mixture to raclette dishes and cook under the heating element for 5–7 minutes until golden brown.

Raclette Trays

Veggie Medley

SERVES 4:

➤ 5 oz cauliflower florets

5 oz broccoli florets

½ cup white wine or stock

½ cup white wine vinegar

2 tbs sugar

½ tsp salt

1 tsp peppercorns

2 tbs sliced almonds

2 tbs currants

7 oz sliced Tilsit

⏱ Prep time: 20 minutes

⏱ Cooking time: 5 minutes

➤ Calories/serving: About 230

1 | Rinse florets and cut into very small pieces. Bring wine, vinegar, 1 cup water, sugar, salt, and peppercorns to a boil. Blanch cauliflower for 2–3 minutes, then add broccoli, cook for another 2–3 minutes, and drain.

2 | Toast almonds until light brown, then combine with currants and florets. Cut cheese to fit raclette dishes.

3 | Distribute vegetables in cooking trays and place cheese on top. Cook for about 5 minutes.

Raclette with Hot Stone

Creamed Spinach with Eggs

SERVES 4:

➤ 3 green onions

9 oz mozzarella

¾ cup creamed spinach (your favorite recipe)

Salt | Pepper

4 small eggs

Hungarian sweet paprika

⏱ Prep time: 10 minutes

⏱ Cooking time: 15 minutes

➤ Calories/serving: About 250

1 | Clean green onions, rinse, and cut into fine rings. Slice mozzarella thinly.

2 | Place a few spoonfuls of cream spinach to fill each tray half full, then place on the preheated hot stone to warm. Season with salt and pepper.

3 | Break open 1 egg on each portion of spinach and let it solidify in the dish for about 7 minutes. Season with paprika. Top with cheese and cook under the heating element for about 7 minutes.

Photo top: **Mixed Mushrooms with Cheese**   *Photo middle:* **Veggie Medley** ➤
Photo bottom: **Creamed Spinach with Eggs**

Raclette Trays
Asparagus Gratin

SERVES 4:

➤ 2 lbs green asparagus

3/4 cup dried tomatoes in oil (4 1/2 oz)

3 tbs bread crumbs

3 1/2 oz freshly grated Parmesan

1 lb boiled potatoes

Salt | Pepper

🕐 Prep time: 25 minutes

🕐 Cooking time: 10 minutes

➤ Calories/serving: About 325

1 | Bring salted water to a boil. Rinse asparagus, peel bottom third, and cut off woody ends. Boil in salted water for 3 minutes, rinse under cold water, and drain well.

2 | Drain tomatoes, setting aside the oil. Cut tomatoes into strips. Cut asparagus on an angle into pieces 1 inch long and mix carefully with tomatoes and oil.

3 | Combine bread crumbs and Parmesan. Slice potatoes, distribute in cooking trays, and season with salt and pepper. Top with asparagus, tomatoes, and cheese-bread crumb mixture. Cook under the heating element for 8–10 minutes.

Raclette Trays
Olive-Tomato Polenta

SERVES 4:

➤ 2 1/2 cups vegetable stock

2/3 cup yellow cornmeal

Salt | Pepper

1/2 pint cherry tomatoes

8 pitted black olives

2 cloves garlic

2 tbs olive oil

1/2 bunch basil

9 oz mozzarella

1 1/2 oz freshly grated Parmesan

Grease for the baking sheet

🕐 Prep time: 40 minutes

🕐 Cooking time: 15 minutes

➤ Calories/serving: About 425

1 | Bring stock to a boil, sprinkle in cornmeal, and cook over low heat for 15 minutes while stirring. Season polenta with salt and pepper and spread half onto a greased baking sheet to a 1/3-inch thickness. Let cool.

2 | Rinse tomatoes and cut into quarters. Cut olives into rings. Peel garlic and slice thinly. Heat oil in a small pan and sauté garlic over low heat for 3 minutes until translucent. Then mix immediately with tomatoes and olives.

3 | Rinse basil and cut into strips. Mix with tomatoes. Slice mozzarella and drain between 2 layers of paper towel.

4 | Cut polenta into 8 pieces (to fit cooking trays) and distribute among trays. Pour tomato mixture over the top, season with salt and pepper, and top with mozzarella. Sprinkle with Parmesan and cook under the heating element for 10–15 minutes.

Raclette Trays

Rosemary-Infused Mediterranean Vegetables

SERVES 4:

➤ 1 eggplant
Salt | Pepper
1/4 cup dried tomatoes in oil (1 1/2 oz)
1 small zucchini
1 tbs lemon juice
3 tbs olive oil
1 clove garlic
7 oz sliced fontina
1 tsp dried rosemary
3 tbs grated Parmesan
Parchment paper for the baking sheet

🕓 Prep time: 30 minutes
🕓 Cooking time: 7 minutes
➤ Calories/serving: About 335

1 | Rinse eggplant, cut into 1/4-inch thick slices, and salt generously. Set aside for 15 minutes. Preheat oven to 350°F. Line a baking sheet with parchment paper.

2 | Rinse off eggplant slices, pat dry, arrange on the baking sheet, and roast in the oven (middle rack) for 15 minutes. Let cool, then slice lengthwise.

3 | In the meantime, chop tomatoes coarsely. Cut zucchini into fine strips. Combine lemon juice, pepper, and oil. Squeeze garlic through a press and add. Cut fontina to fit cooking trays.

4 | Combine everything except fontina in a bowl. Transfer to cooking trays, top with fontina, and cook under the heating element for 5–7 minutes.

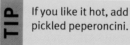

TIP If you like it hot, add pickled peperoncini.

Raclette Trays

Root Vegetable Pancakes

SERVES 4:

➤ 2 medium leeks
2 carrots
1 parsnip
4 tbs crème fraîche
1 tbs lemon juice
7 oz Cheddar
1/4 cup salted, roasted peanuts
Pepper
Oil for the cooking trays

🕓 Prep time: 20 minutes
🕓 Cooking time: 7 minutes
➤ Calories/serving: About 355

1 | Cut leeks in half lengthwise, rinse, and cut crosswise into fine strips. Clean carrots and parsnip, peel, and, using a slicer, vegetable peeler, or very sharp knife, cut lengthwise into narrow slices and then into very fine matchsticks. Stir crème fraîche and lemon juice into vegetables.

2 | Depending on its age, crumble Cheddar, dice finely, or grate coarsely. Chop peanuts. Add both ingredients to the vegetable mixture and season with pepper.

3 | Brush cooking trays with oil, fill with vegetable mixture, and cook under the heating element for 5–7 minutes until the cheese is golden brown.

TIP Blanch vegetable strips briefly and the pancakes will be more tender.

Photo left: Root Vegetable Pancakes   Photo right: Rosemary-Infused Mediterranean Vegetables ➤

Raclette Trays
Zucchini Blossom Rounds

SERVES 4:

➤ **4 zucchini blossoms attached to zucchini**

3½ oz shiitake mushrooms (may substitute white mushrooms)

1 shallot

1 clove garlic

2 tsps fresh thyme leaves (may substitute ½ tsp dried thyme)

1½ tbs butter

7 oz feta

Salt | Pepper

🕐 Prep time: 30 minutes

🕐 Cooking time: 7 minutes

➤ Calories/serving: About 240

1 | Remove blossoms from zucchini and rinse zucchini. Clean mushrooms, wipe with a damp cloth, and dice zucchini and mushrooms very finely.

2 | Peel shallot and garlic, mince, and braise in butter for several minutes along with zucchini, mushrooms, and thyme.

3 | Crumble cheese finely and stir into vegetables. Season to taste with salt and pepper.

4 | Carefully open zucchini blossoms and remove stamens. Fill blossoms with vegetable-cheese mixture but don't fill them too much because the blossoms must have a slender shape. Gently press petals onto the filling on all sides. Place blossoms on a work surface and, using a sharp knife, cut crosswise into ⅓-inch thick slices.

5 | Place zucchini blossom rounds in the cooking trays and cook under the heating element for 5–7 minutes until golden brown.

➤ Side dish: Polenta Diamonds (page 25).

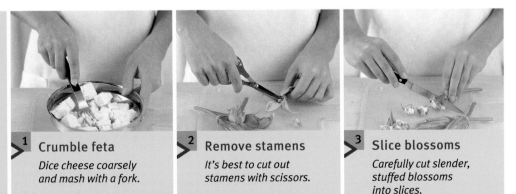

1 Crumble feta
Dice cheese coarsely and mash with a fork.

2 Remove stamens
It's best to cut out stamens with scissors.

3 Slice blossoms
Carefully cut slender, stuffed blossoms into slices.

19

Raclette Trays
Figs with Honey and Peppercorns

SERVES 4:

➤ **8 figs**
   1 tsp pickled green peppercorns
   1 tsp pink peppercorns
   4 tbs honey
   1 tbs orange liqueur
   7 oz Gouda

🕐 Prep time: 10 minutes
🕐 Cooking time: 10 minutes
➤ Calories/serving: About 240

1 | Rinse and dry figs carefully, cut in half lengthwise, and cut into them crosswise without cutting all the way through. Cut a thin slice from the rounded side of each fig so the halves will stay upright.

2 | Drain green peppercorns and chop coarsely with a knife. Crush pink peppercorns slightly with the flat side of a knife blade. Combine honey and orange liqueur. Grate cheese coarsely.

3 | Place 2 fig halves in each cooking tray and sprinkle with cheese. Cook under the heating element for 8–10 minutes. Drizzle with honey and sprinkle with chopped and crushed peppercorns.

Raclette Trays
Diced Mango and Mozzarella

SERVES 4:

➤ **3 balls of mozzarella (4 oz each)**
   5 oz serrano ham
   2 ripe mangos
   1 small red chili pepper
   1 lime
   2½ tbs butter
   Salt

🕐 Prep time: 20 minutes
🕐 Cooking time: 10 minutes
➤ Calories/serving: About 505

1 | Pat mozzarella dry and slice. Drain between 2 layers of paper towel. Cut ham crosswise into strips the thickness of a finger.

2 | Peel mangos. Slice fruit from pit and cut into ⅓-inch cubes. Slit open chili pepper lengthwise, remove seeds, and dice as finely as possible. Rinse lime under hot water, dry, and grate off zest. Squeeze out lime juice and reserve.

3 | In a small pan, melt butter and braise lime zest and chili pepper over low heat for 3 minutes while stirring. Next, mix mangos with 4 tbs reserved lime juice, then blend with chili butter and salt.

4 | Distribute mangos and ham in cooking trays, top with mozzarella, and cook under the heating element for 8–10 minutes.

Meat Dishes

This chapter is full of exciting flavor combinations to please your palate. Try the sophisticated pairing of Duck Breast with Apple Compote, perfect for a cozy fall dinner. Or become addicted to Spicy Chorizo-Chili Raclette.

Spicy Chorizo-Chili Raclette

SERVES 4:

➤ 5 oz chorizo | 5 pickled peperoncini
1 small bunch cilantro
1 (16-oz) can chili beans
Salt | Pepper | 2 tbs oil | 2 cloves garlic
1 cup frozen corn | 9 oz sliced Cheddar

1 | Peel and dice chorizo. Cut peperoncini into rings. Chop cilantro. Combine all these ingredients with beans and season with salt and pepper. In a small pan, heat oil. Squeeze garlic through a press and add to pan along with corn. Braise over medium heat until garlic softens and corn is warm, then add to bean mixture.

2 | Distribute bean mixture in cooking trays, top with cheese, and cook under the heating element for 8–10 minutes.

Turkey Breast with Gorgonzola and Pears

SERVES 4:

➤ 1 lb smoked turkey breast sliced
1/3-inch thick | 1 lb endive
10 oz Gorgonzola | 1 small pear,
peeled, cut into quarters, and cored
1/4 cup chopped almonds
Salt | Cayenne pepper

1 | Dice turkey breast and Gorgonzola. Clean endive, cut in half lengthwise, remove core, and cut into strips 1/3-inch wide. Slice pear, then dice.

2 | Combine turkey breast, endive, pears, and almonds and season with salt and cayenne. Distribute in cooking trays and top with Gorgonzola. Cook under the heating element for 8–10 minutes.

23

Raclette Trays
Zesty Sausage Trays

SERVES 4:

➤ 3 ½ oz chorizo

2 pork sausages

1 large green bell pepper

4 large pickled peperoncini

10 (approx.) pimento-stuffed olives

5 oz manchego

12 (approx.) pickled cocktail onions

🕐 Prep time: 10 minutes

🕐 Cooking time: 10 minutes

➤ Calories/serving: About 345

1 | Peel sausages and cut into thin slices. Rinse bell pepper, clean, and cut into fine strips. Cut up peperoncini and slice olives. Slice cheese.

2 | Place a little sausage, bell pepper, peperoncini, olive, and onion in each raclette dish, cook under the heating element for 5 minutes, then top with cheese and melt under the heating element.

Raclette with Hot Stone
Turkey-Bacon Polenta Diamonds

SERVES 4:

➤ 1 cup hearty vegetable stock

⅔ cup cornmeal

1 ½ oz grated pecorino

1 egg yolk

Salt | Pepper

12 tbs olive oil

1 lb turkey breast sliced paper-thin

2 tbs lemon juice

1 tbs dried sage

5 oz bacon

9 oz mozzarella

🕐 Prep time: 1 hour

🕐 Cooking time: 12 minutes

➤ Calories/serving: About 780

1 | Bring vegetable stock to a boil, stir in cornmeal, and cook over low heat for about 15 minutes while stirring. Let cool slightly.

2 | Stir cheese and egg yolk into polenta and season with salt and pepper. Spread polenta mixture on a cold, greased baking sheet to a thickness of ⅓ inch and refrigerate.

3 | In the meantime, cut turkey slices to fit cooking trays. Combine 8 tbs oil, lemon juice, and sage, distribute over meat, and marinate for about 30 minutes.

4 | Dice bacon and mozzarella finely. Drain mozzarella between paper towels. Scrape as much marinade from the meat as possible.

5 | Brush polenta with 2 tbs oil, cut into small diamonds, reverse these onto a platter, and brush with another 2 tbs oil.

6 | Cook diamonds on the hot stone for at least 5 minutes on each side. Distribute meat and bacon in raclette dishes, sprinkle with cheese, and cook meat until golden brown.

Raclette Trays
Mortadella Melt

SERVES 4:

- ➤ 1 lb small, firm potatoes
- 1 lb mortadella sliced 1/3-inch thick
- 1/3 cup packaged fried onions
- 2 1/2 tbs butter
- Freshly grated nutmeg
- Salt | Pepper
- 10 oz sliced Emmenthaler

⏱ Prep time: 45 minutes
⏱ Cooking time: 10 minutes
➤ Calories/serving: About 735

1 | Rinse potatoes and boil with the peels on in salted water for 20 minutes. In the meantime, cut mortadella into 1/3-inch cubes and mix with fried onions.

2 | Drain potatoes, rinse under cold water, and let cool slightly. Then peel and cut in half lengthwise and crosswise. Melt butter, season with nutmeg, and mix with potatoes. Season with salt and pepper.

3 | Distribute potatoes and mortadella in raclette dishes and cover with Emmenthaler. Cook under the heating element for 8–10 minutes.

Raclette Grill
Sauerkraut-Sausage Raclette

SERVES 4:

- ➤ 1 (16-oz) jar sauerkraut
- 3 onions
- 3 tbs oil
- 1 large red skinned apple
- Salt | Pepper
- 12 small bratwurst
- 10 oz sliced caraway cheese

⏱ Prep time: 30 minutes
⏱ Cooking time: 10 minutes
➤ Calories/serving: About 655

1 | Pour sauerkraut into a colander, rinse under cold water, if desired, and drain well. Peel onions, cut in half lengthwise, and then cut crosswise into half rings 1/4-inch thick. In a pan, heat oil and braise onions for 3 minutes until translucent.

2 | In the meantime, rinse apple, cut into quarters, remove core, and cut quarters crosswise into 1/4-inch thick slices. Add to onions and braise for another 3 minutes. Add sauerkraut, bring to a boil, and season with salt and pepper. Then set aside.

3 | Cut cheese to fit cooking trays or into strips. Sprinkle a little salt on the preheated grill and cook sausages on all sides for 5 minutes. Distribute sauerkraut in raclette dishes. Cut sausages in half and place on top of sauerkraut. Top with cheese and cook under the heating element for 8–10 minutes.

➤ Side dish: Homemade mashed potatoes.

Raclette Grill
Prosciutto-Pumpkin Raclette

SERVES 4:

➤ **10 oz pumpkin flesh**
7 oz prosciutto
7 oz Gruyère
2 medium eggs
$1/3$ cup milk
$1/2$ cup heavy cream
Salt | Pepper
Cayenne pepper
Hungarian sweet paprika
Oil for the cooking trays

🕐 Prep time: 25 minutes
🕐 Cooking time: 10 minutes
➤ Calories/serving: About 585

1 | Cut pumpkin flesh into cubes of about $1/3$ inch. Cook in salted water for 10–15 minutes until al dente, rinse under cold water, and drain well.

2 | Dice prosciutto or cut into strips and mix with pumpkin. Grate cheese coarsely. Transfer both to bowls. Whisk together eggs, milk, and cream, season with salt, pepper, cayenne, and paprika, and place on the table in a gravy boat.

3 | Heat raclette dishes briefly on the preheated grill and brush lightly with oil. Distribute proscuitto-pumpkin mixture in raclette dishes, sprinkle with cheese, and pour some of the egg mixture over the top. Set on the grill for several minutes until the egg has solidified on the bottom, then cook under the heating element until golden brown.

Raclette Trays
Herbed Vegetable-Ground Beef Medley

SERVES 4:

➤ **1 bunch green onions**
1 tbs oil
9 oz ground beef
1 cup frozen corn kernels
$1/4$ tsp dried marjoram
$1/4$ tsp dried thyme
Salt | Pepper
$1/4$ cup dried tomatoes in oil ($1^1/2$ oz)
7 oz sliced Butterkäse

🕐 Prep time: 20 minutes
🕐 Cooking time: 5 minutes
➤ Calories/serving: About 470

1 | Clean and rinse green onions. Cut light green parts into fine rings and dice white parts finely. Place onion greens in a small bowl.

2 | In a pot, heat oil and fry ground meat, chopped onions, and corn while stirring constantly until meat is crumbly and all the liquid has evaporated. Season with marjoram, thyme, salt, and pepper and transfer to a serving bowl.

3 | Cut tomatoes into small pieces. Cut cheese to fit raclette dishes. Arrange all these ingredients separately.

4 | Distribute ground beef mixture in raclette dishes and top with tomatoes, reserved green onions, and, finally, the cheese. Cook under the heating element oven for about 5 minutes.

➤ Variation: Replace ground beef with chopped chicken; brown onions in oil, fry meat until brown, and season as described.

Raclette with Hot Stone
Duck Breast with Apple Compote

SERVES 4:

➤ 1 small piece ginger
1 tbs honey
2 tbs dry sherry
2 tbs oil
9 oz smoked duck breast
7 oz sliced Raclette cheese
2 small apples
$1/4$ cup cranberries
Sugar (optional)
Salt

⏱ Prep time: 25 minutes
⏱ Cooking time: 7 minutes
➤ Calories/serving: About 425

1 | Peel ginger and grate very finely. Combine with honey, sherry, and oil.

2 | Slice duck very thinly, brush with marinade, and set aside. Cut cheese to fit raclette dishes.

3 | In the meantime, peel apples, remove cores, and cut into small pieces. Steam in a little water with the cranberries until tender.

If desired, season apple compote to taste with sugar and transfer to a serving bowl.

4 | Sprinkle preheated hot stone with a little salt and brown duck breast slices on both sides. Distribute in raclette dishes, top with cheese, and cook under the heating element for 5–7 minutes. Serve compote on the side.

Raclette Trays
Chinese Cabbage and Ham

SERVES 4:

➤ 1 cup frozen peas
10 oz Chinese cabbage
9 oz cooked ham in $1/4$-inch thick slices
1 medium tomato, peeled, quartered, and seeded
Salt | Pepper
10 oz Monterey pepper jack cheese

⏱ Prep time: 20 minutes
⏱ Cooking time: 10 minutes
➤ Calories/serving: About 315

1 | Cook peas in boiling water for 1 minute, pour into a colander, rinse under cold water, and drain well. Remove outer leaves from Chinese cabbage. Cut head in half lengthwise and then into strips the width of a finger.

2 | Dice ham and tomatoes, mix with Chinese cabbage and peas, and season generously with salt and pepper. Cut cheese to fit cooking trays.

3 | Distribute Chinese cabbage mixture in raclette dishes and top with cheese. Cook under the heating element for 8–10 minutes.

➤ Variation: Instead of cooked ham, you can also use smoked turkey breast. Or you can use Chinese sausages from an Asian market, sliced and mixed with the Chinese cabbage.

Photo top: **Duck Breast with Apple Compote**   *Photo bottom:* **Chinese Cabbage and Ham** ➤

Seafood Raclette

For dining on the lighter side, fish and shellfish are always welcome on the menu. Exotic combinations such as mango and shrimp will tickle your taste buds, or try the classic pairing of dill and cod served with a cheddar sauce for a slightly unconventional but tasty twist.

Mango Shrimp

SERVES 4:

➤ 2 tsps green peppercorns
10 oz frozen shrimp, thawed and
drained | 3 tbs oil | 2 tbs lemon juice
1 small mango | Salt | Sugar
¼ cup sliced almonds

1 | Crush peppercorns. Combine shrimp,
peppercorns, oil, and lemon juice. Peel
mango, cut fruit from pit, and dice finely.
Add diced mango to shrimp and season
mixture to taste with salt and sugar.

2 | Place a little shrimp-mango mixture
in the raclette dishes and cook for about
8 minutes, adding sliced almonds toward
the end.

Savory Sardines with Bell Peppers

SERVES 4:

➤ 3 sardines packed in oil, drained
1 large yellow bell pepper
1 shallot | 1 clove garlic
3 tbs finely chopped parsley
Salt | Pepper | 7 oz pecorino

1 | Cut up sardines coarsely. Rinse bell
pepper, clean, and dice very finely. Peel
shallot and garlic and mince. Combine
shallot, garlic, parsley, and bell pepper.
Season with salt and pepper. Grate
cheese and place cheese, fish, and
vegetables on the table.

2 | Distribute sardines and vegetable
mixture in raclette dishes, sprinkle
with cheese, and cook until cheese
is golden brown.

33

Raclette Trays

Provencal Tuna with Basil Oil

SERVES 4:

- ➤ 2 (6-oz) cans tuna packed in water

  3 balls mozzarella (4 oz each)

  1½ lbs firm, ripe tomatoes

  1 bunch basil

  8 tbs olive oil

  4 green onions

  2 tsps pickled green peppercorns

  Salt

Prep time: 30 minutes

Cooking time: 10 minutes

➤ Calories/serving: About 515

1 | Drain tuna. Pat mozzarella dry, cut into ⅓-inch cubes, and drain between 2 layers of paper towel.

2 | Pour boiling water over tomatoes, let stand briefly, rinse under cold water, and peel. Cut tomatoes in half, remove seeds, and dice flesh finely. Drain on paper towels.

3 | Rinse basil, shake dry, remove leaves, and purée with oil. Mix one half with the tomatoes and the other half with the mozzarella.

4 | Clean green onions, rinse, and cut into fine rings. Using a large knife, coarsely chop peppercorns and combine with tomatoes and onions. Pull apart tuna with a fork.

5 | Distribute tomatoes in raclette dishes and salt lightly. Top with tuna and mozzarella and cook under the heating element for 8–10 minutes.

Raclette Trays

Dilled Cod with Cheddar Sauce

SERVES 4:

- ➤ 3 slices mixed-grain bread (about 5 oz)

  2 tbs butter

  2 tbs oil

  1 cup frozen peas

  1⅓ lbs skinless cod filet

  2 tbs lemon juice

  3 tsps hot mustard

  ½ bunch chopped dill

  1 cup fish stock

  9 oz mascarpone

  4½ oz grated Cheddar

  Salt | Pepper

Prep time: 35 minutes

Cooking time: 10 minutes

➤ Calories/serving: About 780

1 | Cut bread into ⅓-inch cubes. In a pan, heat butter and oil and toast bread until crispy while stirring constantly, then let cool. Pour boiling water over peas, drain, rinse under cold water, and drain again.

2 | Pat cod dry and cut into ⅓-inch cubes. Combine lemon juice, mustard, and dill and mix with fish and peas.

3 | Bring fish stock to a boil and remove from heat. Stir in mascarpone and Cheddar and season with salt and pepper.

4 | Distribute fish and bread cubes in raclette dishes. Top with cheese sauce and cook under the heating element for 6–10 minutes until the sauce is slightly brown.

Raclette Grill
Potato-Crusted Pollock

SERVES 4:

- ➤ 1 lb pollock filet
  Salt | Pepper
  2 tbs lemon juice
  9 oz potatoes
  12 (approx.) pitted olives
  ³/₄ cup heavy cream
  1 tsp herbes de Provence
  1 tbs olive oil

🕐 Prep time: 35 minutes
🕐 Cooking time: 15 minutes
➤ Calories/serving: About 295

1 | Cut fish into strips about ¹/₃-inch thick and season with salt, pepper, and lemon juice. Cover and set aside.

2 | Peel potatoes, cut up coarsely, and cook in salted water for about 20 minutes until tender. In the meantime, chop olives.

3 | Heat cream. Drain potatoes, let cool slightly, and mash. Stir in cream and season to taste with salt, pepper, and herbes de Provence.

4 | Gently pat fish strips dry and combine with olive oil. Distribute in raclette dishes and cook on the preheated grill for about 10 minutes, turning fish once. Top with potatoes and cook under the heating element until golden brown.

Raclette Trays
Herbed Mussels

SERVES 4:

- ➤ 1 shallot
  1 clove garlic
  2 tbs butter
  1 tbs dried Italian herb mixture
  ¹/₂ cup frozen peas
  1 tbs flour
  ³/₄ cup milk
  4 tbs grated Parmesan
  1 tsp hot mustard
  Salt | White pepper
  9 oz canned mussels

🕐 Prep time: 20 minutes
🕐 Cooking time: 8 minutes
➤ Calories/serving: About 170

1 | Peel shallot and garlic, chop finely, and sauté in butter along with herbs and peas until shallot is translucent and peas soften. Stir in flour until it foams up. Let cool slightly, then add milk.

2 | Bring sauce to a boil while stirring constantly and thicken over medium heat. Remove from heat, stir in Parmesan and mustard, and season to taste with salt and pepper.

3 | Drain mussels and stir into sauce. Transfer to a serving bowl.

4 | Place a little of the mussel mixture in each raclette dish and cook under the heating element for 6–8 minutes until golden brown.

TIP The sauce will taste even finer if you replace some of the milk with mussel juice.

Raclette Trays

Bread Crumb-Crusted Monkfish

SERVES 4:

➤ 4 tbs horseradish

9 tbs softened herb butter with lemon

$1/2$ cup bread crumbs

Salt | Pepper

$1^1/_3$ lbs skinless monkfish filet

2 leeks

7 oz freshly grated fontina

🕐 Prep time: 40 minutes

🕐 Cooking time: 10 minutes

➤ Calories/serving: About 630

1 | Peel horseradish and mince with an onion chopper or grate. Knead together with butter and bread crumbs and season with salt and pepper.

2 | Cut monkfish into slices $3/4$-inch thick and sprinkle with salt and pepper on all sides. Distribute bread crumb mixture on fish, press on well, and refrigerate.

3 | Clean leeks and cut into rings $1/4$-inch thick. Blanch in boiling salted water for 2 minutes, drain, and rinse under cold water. Drain and mix with cheese.

4 | Distribute leek and fish pieces in raclette dishes and cook under the heating element for 8–10 minutes.

Raclette Trays

Flounder over Spinach and Tomatoes

SERVES 4:

➤ 2 lbs young spinach leaves

1 lb tomatoes

1 bunch green onions

4 tbs olive oil

Salt | Pepper

1 lb skinless flounder filet

2 tbs lemon juice

1 tbs lemon zest

7 oz freshly grated smoked cheese

🕐 Prep time: 45 minutes

🕐 Cooking time: 10 minutes

➤ Calories/serving: About 385

1 | Rinse spinach thoroughly. Remove thick stems. Place wet spinach in a large pot, cover, and wilt over high heat for 5 minutes.

2 | Pour boiling water over tomatoes, let stand briefly, rinse under cold water, and peel. Cut tomatoes in half, remove seeds, and chop flesh coarsely. Clean green onions, rinse, and cut into fine rings, including tender green parts.

3 | Squeeze out spinach thoroughly in a dishtowel and chop coarsely. Heat olive oil and braise onions for 2 minutes. Add tomatoes and spinach and season with salt and pepper. Cover and braise over low heat for 5 minutes.

4 | Pat flounder dry and cut into $3/4$-inch-wide strips. Combine with lemon juice and zest and season with salt and pepper.

5 | Distribute spinach in raclette dishes, top with fish, and sprinkle with cheese. Cook under the preheated heating element for 8–10 minutes.

From the Grill

For a sizzling good time, gather up a group of friends and try any of these recipes designed for your raclette grill top. The flavors here span the globe, from all-American Cheddar burgers to southeast Asian Chicken Tenders with Peanut Dip.

Zucchini Coins with Yogurt Dip

SERVES 4:

➤ 1½ oz feta | ¾ cup yogurt | 2 tbs oil
1 tbs lime juice | 1 clove garlic
4 tbs chopped cilantro
Salt | Pepper | 1 lb zucchini

1 | Mash feta finely and mix with yogurt and oil. Stir in lime juice, garlic squeezed through a press, and cilantro. Season yogurt dip with salt and pepper.

2 | Rinse zucchini, clean, and cut into slices no more than ¼-inch thick. Sprinkle preheated grill with a little salt and cook zucchini until golden brown on both sides. Season with pepper if desired and serve with the dip.

Seafood Crostini

SERVES 4:

➤ 2 sole filets | 2 slices salmon filet (1½ oz each) | 1½ oz small raw shrimp, peeled and deveined | 4 tbs lemon juice
½ baguette | 3 tbs herb butter
4 plum tomatoes | 3 tbs oil
Salt | Pepper | ½ cup crème fraîche

1 | Cut fish pieces in half and sprinkle with lemon juice, along with shrimp. Slice bread and spread with herb butter. Slice tomatoes, remove seeds, and brush with oil. Pat fish and shrimp dry and brush with oil.

2 | Sprinkle preheated grill with salt. Grill tomatoes, fish, shrimp, and bread and season with pepper. Top bread with all ingredients and serve with crème fraîche.

41

Raclette Grill

Bacon-Wrapped Dried Fruit Skewers

SERVES 4:

➤ 7 oz bacon

4 tbs sweet hot chili sauce

24 dried apricots

24 prunes

Wooden skewers

🕐 Prep time: 25 minutes

🕐 Cooking time: 6 minutes

➤ Calories/serving: About 445

1 | Cut bacon slices in half crosswise and cut into 24 pieces of about equal size. Lay these out side by side and spread a thin layer of chili sauce on top. Place 1 prune or apricot on each piece of bacon and roll up.

2 | Alternately thread apricots and prunes onto 2 parallel skewers (so the fruit won't rotate when you turn the skewer). Cook skewers on the preheated grill for 6 minutes, turning occasionally.

➤ Variation: Bacon skewers also taste great with fresh dates. First cut open dates lengthwise and remove pits.

Raclette Grill

Eggplant Pesto Rolls

SERVES 4:

➤ 3 eggplant (2 lbs)

Salt | Pepper

2 bunches basil

3 cloves garlic

1 tbs sunflower seeds

3½ oz feta

8 tbs olive oil

¼ cup bread crumbs

1 cup low-fat sour cream

½ cup yogurt

1 cucumber

3 sprigs mint

Wooden skewers

🕐 Prep time: 1 hour and 20 minutes

🕐 Cooking time: 20 minutes

➤ Calories/serving: About 435

1 | Clean eggplant and, using a vegetable slicer, cut lengthwise into slices ⅛-inch thick. Lay slices flat on a rack, salt, and set aside for 1 hour.

2 | In the meantime, rinse basil and pat dry. Remove leaves and chop finely. Peel garlic. In an ungreased pan, roast sunflower seeds until light brown while stirring constantly, then remove from pan. Dice feta.

3 | In a blender, process basil, 2 cloves garlic, sunflower seeds, feta, and 4 tbs olive oil to make a smooth paste. Add bread crumbs and season the pesto mixture with salt and pepper.

4 | Stir together sour cream and yogurt until smooth. Squeeze garlic through a press and add, then season with salt and pepper. Peel cucumber in a striped pattern, remove seeds, and grate. Fold into sour cream-yogurt mixture and season to taste. Rinse mint, remove leaves, and chop. Fold into dip.

5 | Pat eggplant dry, spread with pesto, roll up, and brush the outside with oil. Thread rolls onto skewers. Cook on the preheated grill for 15–20 minutes. Serve with the sour cream dip.

Raclette Grill

Chicken Tenders with Peanut Dip

SERVES 4:

➤ 1 skinned double chicken breast

3 tbs teriyaki marinade

Salt | Pepper

➤ For the peanut dip:

$1/2$ cup unsweetened peanut butter

$1/2$ cup chicken stock (add more as needed to achieve desired consistency)

2 tbs dry sherry (optional)

2 green onions

2 fresh red chili peppers

Salt

🕐 Prep time: 1 hour and 15 minutes

🕐 Cooking time: 10 minutes

➤ Calories/serving: About 330

1 | Debone chicken breast and cut into two filets. Cut each of these in half length-wise, place between 2 pieces of plastic wrap, and flatten slightly with a rolling pin. Drizzle with marinade, cover, and refrigerate for 1 hour.

2 | For the dip, stir together peanut butter, stock, and sherry. Clean green onions and chop finely. Rinse chili peppers, clean, and chop finely. Add onions and chilies to dip and season with salt.

3 | Cook meat on the preheated grill for about 10 minutes, turning once. Season with salt and pepper. Serve with the peanut dip.

Raclette Grill

Burgers with Arugula Cream

SERVES 4:

➤ For the patties:

1 stale roll

1 lemon

1 shallot

$1/2$ tsp dried marjoram

$1/2$ tsp dried thyme

1 egg

$3/4$ lb ground meat of your choice

1 clove garlic

Salt | Pepper

3 tbs olive oil

➤ For the arugula cream:

$1 1/2$ oz arugula

$1/2$ cup sour cream

3 tbs yogurt

Salt | Cayenne pepper

1 pinch sugar

🕐 Prep time: 35 minutes

🕐 Cooking time: 12 minutes

➤ Calories/serving: About 435

1 | Soak roll in water. Rinse lemon under hot water and remove no more than 1 tsp zest. Squeeze juice from one-half for the arugula cream. Peel shallot and mince.

2 | Squeeze out roll thoroughly and combine in a bowl with lemon zest, herbs, egg, and ground meat. Peel garlic, squeeze through a press, and add. Knead well and season generously with salt and pepper. With moistened hands, shape into burgers with 2 inch diameters and not too thick. Brush with oil.

3 | For the cream, sort arugula, rinse, dry, and chop finely. Stir together sour cream and yogurt until creamy and season to taste with cayenne, salt, sugar, and lemon juice, then fold in arugula.

4 | Cook burgers on the preheated grill for about 12 minutes, turning as needed. Serve with arugula cream.

Raclette Grill
Shrimp Skewers with Herb Sauce

SERVES 4:

- **32 frozen jumbo shrimp, raw and peeled**
- **2 limes**
- **4 tbs soy sauce**
- **7 tbs oil**
- **1 clove garlic**
- **Cayenne pepper**
- **1 bunch chives**
- **1 bunch Italian parsley**
- **1/2 bunch lemon balm**
- **Salt | Pepper**
- **16 wooden skewers**

⏱ Prep time: 1 hour and 30 minutes

⏱ Cooking time: 8 minutes

➤ Calories/serving: About 320

1 | Thaw shrimp. Rinse limes under hot water. Cover the base of a grater with parchment paper and grate lime zest onto the paper. Remove paper and scrape off zest with the back of a knife blade.

2 | Squeeze juice from limes. Combine 6 tbs lime juice, lime zest, soy sauce, and 4 tbs oil. Peel garlic, squeeze through a press, and add. Season with cayenne. Pat shrimp dry, slit open backs with a small knife, and remove the black veins.

3 | Thread 4 shrimp onto eight sets of 2 parallel skewers (so the shrimp won't rotate when you turn the skewers). Place skewers in a bowl and pour marinade over the top. Marinate skewers for 1 hour, turning occasionally.

4 | In the meantime, rinse herbs and shake dry. Cut chives into fine rings. Chop parsley and lemon balm leaves. Combine 2 tbs lime juice, salt, and pepper. Stir in 3 tbs oil and fold in herbs.

5 | Scrape as much marinade off the skewers as possible and cook on the preheated grill for 6–8 minutes, turning once. Serve skewers with herb sauce.

1 ▶ Grate off zest
Place parchment paper under the grater and grate off zest from all sides of the limes.

2 ▶ Devein shrimp
Slit shrimp lengthwise down the back and carefully remove veins.

3 ▶ Thread shrimp
Thread 4 shrimp onto 2 parallel wooden skewers.

Raclette with Hot Stone
Cheddar Burgers

SERVES 4:

- 2 small pickling cucumbers
- 1 small onion
- ½ cup ketchup
- Salt | Pepper
- Tabasco
- 1 lb ground steak
- 2 tbs Worcestershire sauce
- 1 medium egg
- 2 tbs oil
- 4 English muffins
- 7 oz sliced Cheddar

- Prep time: 30 minutes
- Cooking time: 15 minutes
- Calories/serving: About 660

1 | Thinly slice one of the cucumbers and dice the other. Peel onion, dice finely, and mix with diced cucumber and ketchup. Season with salt and 2–3 dashes Tabasco.

2 | Knead together ground steak, Worcestershire sauce, salt, pepper, and egg. Shape this mixture into 8 flat burgers (diameter of about ¾ inch), brush with oil, and cook on the preheated stone on both sides for 8–10 minutes.

3 | Cut apart muffins and toast in raclette dishes under the heating element for 3 minutes until crispy. On each half, place 1 tbs ketchup sauce, some cucumber slices, and one grilled burger. Top with cheese.

4 | Place burgers in raclette dishes and cook in the raclette oven for 5 minutes.

Raclette Grill
Pork Skewers in Grappa Marinade

SERVES 4:

- 10 finely crushed peppercorns
- 10 finely crushed coriander seeds
- 3 tbs plus 1 tsp grappa
- 3 tbs plus 1 tsp olive oil
- 1 lb pork cutlets
- 6 oz Gorgonzola
- 4 shallots
- 2 (6-oz) jars artichokes in oil, drained
- 4 long, paper-thin slices of streaky bacon
- Salt | White pepper
- 8 skewers

- Prep time: 1 hour and 15 minutes
- Cooking time: 12 minutes
- Calories/serving: About 445

1 | Mix seasonings with grappa and olive oil. Cut pork into bite-size pieces, roll around in marinade, cover, and refrigerate for at least 1 hour. Place cheese for vegetables in the freezer and let freeze slightly.

2 | Peel shallots, cut in half lengthwise, and divide into layers. Slice cheese and arrange cheese and artichokes in serving bowls.

3 | Cut bacon in half lengthwise. Pat pork dry and alternately thread pork, shallots, and bacon onto skewers, threading the bacon in a zigzag pattern.

4 | Sprinkle salt on the preheated grill and cook skewers for 10–12 minutes, turning as needed.

5 | Place artichokes in raclette dishes, season lightly with salt and generously with pepper, top with cheese, and cook under the heating element.

Served with...

Looking for a matching salad or a quick sauce to accompany your raclette meal? This chapter offers fantastic recipes that can be served together or separately from raclette and grill dishes.

Crispy Herb-Butter Bread

SERVES 4:

➤ 3 sprigs thyme | 1 small sprig rosemary
½ bunch parsley | 1 clove garlic
7 tbs butter | Salt | Pepper
1 baguette or ciabatta

1 | Preheat oven to 400°F. Rinse herbs, shake dry, pull off leaves, and chop. Peel garlic and squeeze through a press. Mash butter with a fork, then mix in herbs and garlic. Season with salt and pepper.

2 | Slice bread, spread with herb butter, and bake in the oven (bottom rack) for 8–10 minutes.

Tomato Salad with Dill

SERVES 4:

➤ 1½ lbs firm ripe tomatoes | 3 onions
1 bunch dill | Salt | Pepper
5 tbs lemon juice | 2 tbs honey
4 tbs sunflower oil

1 | Rinse tomatoes and cut into ¾-inch cubes. Peel onions and cut into strips. Rinse dill, shake dry, and chop tips. Combine tomatoes, onions, and dill and season with salt and pepper.

2 | Combine lemon juice and honey. Mix in oil using a wire whisk, pour over the salad, and serve.

Tomato Nut Sauce

MAKES ABOUT 1¼ CUPS:

- ➤ 4 tomatoes
  1 small chili pepper
  2 cloves garlic
  1 slice white sandwich bread
  3 tbs ground almonds
  3 tbs ground hazelnuts
  4 tbs olive oil
  Salt
  Red wine vinegar

- ⏱ Prep time: 30 minutes
- ➤ Total calories: About 930

1 | Pour boiling water over tomatoes, rinse under cold water, peel, and remove seeds. Chop flesh, heat in a pot, and reduce while stirring.

2 | In the meantime, slit chili pepper open lengthwise, remove seeds, rinse out the interior, and chop. Peel garlic and chop finely. Dice bread and toast in an ungreased pan while stirring. Add and briefly toast almonds and hazelnuts.

3 | In a blender, purée all these ingredients to make a smooth paste while slowly adding oil. Season to taste with salt and pepper.

- ➤ Serve with: fish, meat, poultry, and cooked vegetables prepared on the grill.

Egg Herb Sauce

MAKES ABOUT ¾ CUP:

- ➤ 4 medium eggs
  3 tbs white wine vinegar
  1 tsp hot mustard
  ½ bunch mixed fresh herbs and ½ bunch chives
  1 shallot
  1 large pickling cucumber
  1 tsp pickled green peppercorns
  3 tbs plus 1 tsp olive oil
  Salt

- ⏱ Prep time: 15 minutes
- ➤ Total calories: About 650

1 | Hard boil eggs, rinse under cold water, and peel. Remove yolks and purée along with vinegar and mustard. Rinse fresh herbs, shake dry, pull off leaves, and chop finely. Mix into egg yolk purée.

2 | Peel shallot and finely dice shallot and cucumber. Finely chop peppercorns. Add all these ingredients to the egg yolk purée. Add oil in a thin stream while beating vigorously and season sauce to taste with salt.

- ➤ Serve with: fish and seafood prepared on the grill but also as a dressing for a green salad (thinned, if necessary).

 TIP Chop egg whites and mix into the sauce.

Photo top: **Tomato Nut Sauce** *Photo bottom:* **Egg Herb Sauce** ➤

Romaine Salad with Radishes

SERVES 4:

- **2 very small heads romaine lettuce**
  1 bunch radishes
  3 1/2 oz fresh goat cheese
  1/2 cup yogurt
  2 tbs lemon juice
  Salt | Pepper
  1 bunch chives
  1 clove garlic
  2 slices mixed-grain bread (3 1/2 oz)
  2 tbs oil
  1 1/2 tbs butter

Prep time: 25 minutes
- Calories/serving: About 240

1 | Rinse lettuce and cut into strips the width of a finger. Clean radishes, rinse, and cut into quarters or eighths.

2 | In a blender, combine goat cheese, yogurt, and lemon juice well and season with salt and pepper. Rinse chives, shake dry, cut into fine rings, and fold into the dressing.

3 | Peel garlic. Remove crust from bread and cut into 1/3-inch cubes. In a pan, heat butter and oil and add garlic squeezed through a press. Sauté bread over medium heat while stirring until golden brown.

4 | Toss lettuce and radishes with the dressing and sprinkle with croutons.

Potato-Radicchio Salad

SERVES 4:

- **1 3/4 lbs small firm potatoes**
  Salt | Pepper
  1 bunch green onions
  1 cup vegetable stock
  1 tsp sugar
  1 tsp lemon zest
  7 tbs white wine vinegar
  2 medium egg yolks
  6 tbs oil
  1 head radicchio

Prep time: 1 hour and 15 minutes
- Calories/serving: About 335

1 | Rinse potatoes. With the peels on, place in salted water, cover, bring to a boil, and simmer over low heat for 15–20 minutes.

2 | In the meantime, clean green onions, rinse, cut light green parts into fine rings, cover, and set aside. Dice white parts finely. Bring stock to a boil with sugar, lemon zest, and diced onion. Stir in vinegar. Whisk egg yolks, stir into stock, and heat but don't let it boil. Stir in oil, salt, and pepper.

3 | Drain potatoes, rinse under cold water, and let cool slightly. Then peel and cut into 1/4-inch thick slices, dropping them directly into the hot marinade. Marinate for 30 minutes.

4 | Rinse radicchio, cut lengthwise into quarters, remove core, and then cut into strips the width of a finger. Fold into potato salad and sprinkle with onion rings.

Mâche with Baked Squash

SERVES 4:

- ➤ 1 kabocha squash (about 1¼ lbs)
- 2 cloves garlic
- Salt | Cayenne pepper
- 4 tbs olive oil
- 2 tbs lemon zest
- 5 tbs lemon juice
- 2 tsps honey
- 3 tbs pumpkin seed oil
- 10½ oz mushrooms
- 4 green onions
- 3½ oz mâche salad (may use arugula)
- Parchment paper

🕐 Prep time: 45 minutes

➤ Calories/serving: About 235

1 | Preheat oven to 425°F. Cut squash in half and scrape out soft interior and seeds with a spoon. Cut into ¾-inch thick wedges and peel. Peel garlic and squeeze through a press. Combine garlic, salt, cayenne pepper, and olive oil.

2 | Cover a baking sheet with parchment paper. Place squash wedges on top and brush with the seasoned oil. Bake in the oven for 25 minutes, turning after 15 minutes and brushing the other side with seasoned oil.

3 | In the meantime, combine lemon zest, lemon juice, and honey and season with salt and 1 pinch cayenne. Mix in pumpkin seed oil.

4 | Clean mushrooms and cut into slices of a uniform thickness. Clean green onions, rinse, and cut into fine rings, including tender green parts. Combine mushrooms, onions, and 4 tbs of the pumpkin seed oil marinade.

5 | Clean mâche, rinse, and spin dry. Arrange squash on a platter, distribute mushrooms and mâche on top, and drizzle with remaining pumpkin seed oil marinade.

1 Prepare squash
Cut squash halves into wedges and then peel wedges.

2 Cut up mushrooms
This is easy to do using an egg slicer.

3 Clean mâche salad
Remove roots, rinse, and spin dry.

The Raclette Party

The main attraction at a raclette party is the variety of ingredients and individual dishes that each guest can prepare in his or her own raclette cooking dish. This also makes raclette an ideal meal for children because they can select the foods they like best. Not to mention, children love to take part in the actual cooking. But make sure an adult sits next to each child, both to help and to keep an eye on the hot utensils.

For a raclette dinner party, table decorations should be kept to a minimum. The table will already be full enough with buffet plates, the appliance itself, and the different bowls of ingredients. You also have to be able to pass the ingredients around and set them down again. So pay attention to selecting the right utensils rather than to fancy decorations.

Have fun cooking with your friends!

✗ **Timing**
As experienced cooks know, the most important thing is to begin your preparations far enough ahead, especially if you want to throw a larger raclette party without getting too stressed.

✗ **Equipment**
Theoretically, a raclette machine with 8 dishes is adequate for 8 guests, but then you have to plan on the meal taking a relatively long time since each guest has access to only 1 dish. As an alternative, you might want to consider borrowing a second raclette machine or buying a second set of raclette dishes.

✗ **Raclette Recipes**
For 8 people, plan on using 2–3 recipes from this book, plus a sufficient quantity of potatoes, another filling side dish, and 2 salads.

✗ **Thirst Quenchers**
Keep in mind that you can never have too much water. Water is the best thing for quenching thirst. If that's too boring, mix sparkling water with a little of your favorite fruit juice. If serving sparking water, count on at least 1 bottle per person.

✗ **Drinks for Pleasure**
If you serve wine, plan on 2 bottles for 3 people. If you prefer beer, you can get a small keg from a liquor store that they will provide chilled. If you serve bottled beer, plan on at least 2 (but preferably 3) bottles per person.

Just Plain Good

Steamy-hot boiled potatoes are the ideal side dish for your creations in raclette dishes. They can be combined with almost anything, are the perfect complement to cheese, and are easily kept warm on a platter during the meal.

1

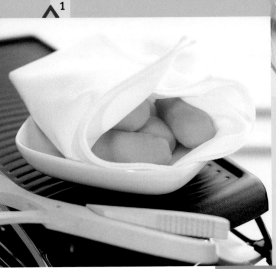

² Cheers!

The type of drinks you provide (in addition to a sufficient amount of water) mainly depend on the preferences of your guests. As a general rule, beer goes best with hearty raclette dishes and wine goes best with more sophisticated, finely seasoned dishes.

Dinner is Served

3

If well planned and prepared far enough in advance, a raclette meal can also be a pleasure for the host, who won't have to be running back and forth to the kitchen.

ABBREVIATIONS
lb = pound
oz = ounce
tsp = teaspoon
tbs = tablespoon

The Author

Claudia Schmidt lives in Munich and works as an independent food scientist in areas ranging from consumer guidance to peer training, and as an author and reader of books on cooking and nutrition.

The Photographer

Kai Mewes is an independent food photographer in Munich who works for publishers and in advertising. Food styling by Daniel Petri.

Photo Credits

Michael Brauner, Karlsruhe: cover photo
Stockfood Eising: pages 4, 7 (2nd photo from left)
Foodfotographie Teubner: pages 6, 7
All others: Kai Mewes, Munich
Additional photography courtesy of Swissmar

Published originally under the title Raclette: neue Rezepte © 2002 Gräfe und Unzer Verlag GmbH, Munich. English language rights for North America © 2002, Silverback Books, Inc.

Editors: Elizabeth Penn, Birgit Rademacker, and Nancy Whitmore
Typesetting and production: Patty Holden and Verlagssatz Linger
Layout and typography: Independent Medien Design, Munich

Printed in Korea

ISBN 1-930603-70-3

Enjoy Other Quick & Easy Books

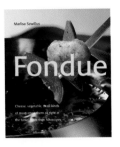

Marlisa Szwillus

Fondue

Cheese, vegetable, meat, all kinds of meat—everything at right at the table—more than 50 recipes

Cornelia Adam

Salads

An array of salads for use as appetizers, delicacies, and party dishes, including simple choices and cutting-edge alternatives.

Sandwiches

Sophisticated, easy fresh food including many delicious combinations of breads, spreads, and fillings.

Xenia Burgtorf

Cornelia Adam

Quiche

Delicious, savory pies with vegetables, meat, poultry or fish—serve for all occasions.

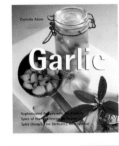

Cornelia Adam

Garlic

Sophisticated Recipes with the Exotic Spice of the Mediterranean Region Spicy (tangy), Fine (delicate), International

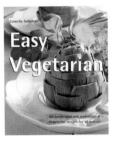

Cornelia Schinharl

Easy Vegetarian

Uncomplicated and sophisticated—Vegetarian recipes for all seasons

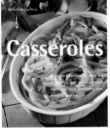

Sebastian Dickhaut

Casseroles

Enjoy casseroles every day of the week, that's a healthy choice—Flavorful and fun.

Annette Heisch

Oil & Vinegar

A wonderful source of information, delicious recipes and helpful hints—liven up your favorite dishes and create tasty sauces and dressings.

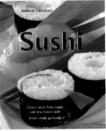

Andreas Fürtmayr

Sushi

Classic ideas from Japan and new fusion sushi Home-made perfectly

1 Noodle, 50 Sauces

Everyday Pasta • Old and New Italian Dishes Noodle biography • 50 Tips for Success

Healthy Wok

Elisabeth Döpp
Christian Willrich
Joerg Behre

Great for light and satisfying meals

Antje Gruener

Grilling

Crisp, flavorful and full-bodied skin morsels from the grill for you or your food, from spareribs to skewered vegetables with sauces and chutneys.

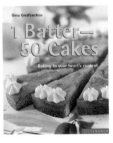

Gina Greifenstein

1 Batter—50 Cakes

Baking to your heart's content

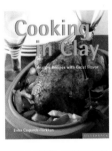

Cooking in Clay

Healthy Recipes with Great Flavor

Erika Casparek-Türkkan

Doris Muliar

Cocktails for Drivers

100% Enjoyment

Antipasti and Tapas

Mediterranean Appetizers
Cornelia Schinharl

Soups

Classic to Contemporary

Sebastian Dickhaut

Claudia Schmidt

Raclette

New Recipes with Cheese, Primer and Party Dips

RACLETTE/GRILL COMBO
- For many of these recipes—and not just those in the chapter dedicated to the grill—you need a raclette/grill or a raclette with hot stone.

Guaranteed Success with Raclette

COOKING WITH RACLETTE DISHES INSIDE
- Never overfill the raclette dishes. Instead, cook more, smaller servings. If you pile the ingredients too high, they won't cook evenly during the brief cooking time and the cheese will brown too quickly because it's too close to the heating elements—or it may even stick to them.

LEFTOVER CHEESE
- Leftover hard and firm cheese can be frozen. Once again, place a piece of waxed or baking paper between the individual slices.
- Leftover cheese is also good for melts, sandwiches, vegetable dishes, soufflés, and sauces. If you don't pack it too tightly together, it will keep in the refrigerator for over a week.

BEFORE AND AFTER
- A plain green salad with a light dressing is an ideal starter for a raclette meal because it can be eaten while the raclette machine is heating up. You're better off serving heartier salads as side dishes with the meal so guests won't get filled up beforehand. You can then finish up with a light fruit salad or even a cold fruit sorbet.